BIG
BIG MOUTHS

by Catherine Ipcizade

Consulting Editor: Gail Saunders-Smith, PhD

Consultant: Tanya Dewey, PhD
University of Michigan Museum of Zoology

CAPSTONE PRESS
a capstone imprint

Pebble Plus is published by Capstone Press,
151 Good Counsel Drive, P.O. Box 669, Mankato, Minnesota 56002.
www.capstonepress.com

092009
005618CGS10

 Books published by Capstone Press are manufactured with paper containing at least 10 percent post-consumer waste.

Library of Congress Cataloging-in-Publication Data
Ipcizade, Catherine.
    Big mouths / by Catherine Ipcizade.
    p. cm. — (Pebble Plus. Big)
    Includes bibliographical references and index.
    Summary: "Simple text and colorful photographs describe the big mouths of nine animals" — Provided by publisher.
    ISBN 978-1-4296-3996-5 (library binding)
    1. Mouth — Juvenile literature. I. Title. II. Series.
QL857.I63 2010
591.4 — dc22   2009026049

Editorial credits
Erika L. Shores, editor; Ted Williams, designer; Wanda Winch, media researcher; Eric Manske, production specialist

Photo credits
Alamy/Michael Doolittle, 7
AnimalsAnimals-Earth Scenes/Michael Dick, 9
CORBIS/Royalty-Free, 5
Digital Vision (Getty Images), cover
Getty Images Inc./Lonely Planet Images/Mark Newman, 11; National Geographic/Paul Nicklen, 21
Minden Pictures/NPL/Anup Shah, 15
Shutterstock/Craig Dingle, 13; designalldone, cover (background); Marina Cano Trueba, 1; Timothy Craig Lubcke, 19
www.marinethemes.com/Mark Conlin, 17

Note to Parents and Teachers

The Big set supports national science standards related to life science. This book describes and illustrates big mouths. The images support early readers in understanding the text. The repetition of words and phrases helps early readers learn new words. This book also introduces early readers to subject-specific vocabulary words, which are defined in the Glossary section. Early readers may need assistance to read some words and to use the Table of Contents, Glossary, Read More, Internet Sites, and Index sections of the book.

Table of Contents

Big

Mouths chomp, scoop,
and roar.
Big mouths help animals
stay alive.

Size:
Most bears can open their mouths
6 inches (15 centimeters).

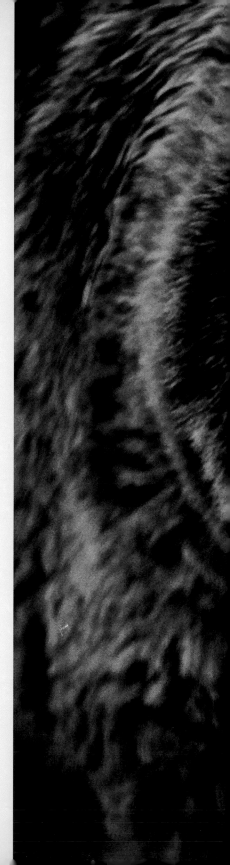

Amazon horned frogs are
big eaters.
They eat any animal
that fits in their big mouths.

Size:

An Amazon horned frog's mouth
is 7.5 inches (19 centimeters) wide.

King cobras open
their big mouths wide.
Cobras can take one hour
to swallow food whole.

Size:
A king cobra fang is up to
0.5 inch (1.3 centimeters) long.

Bigger

Giant anteaters poke
their big snouts into holes.
Their long, sticky tongues
pull out ants.

Size:

A giant anteater's snout is
18 inches (46 centimeters) long.

Pelicans use a big throat
pouch like a fishing net.
The birds scoop up fish to eat.

Size:

A pelican's bill is 14 inches
(36 centimeters) long.

13

A male lion's mouth
lets out big roars.
Other animals know
to stay away.

Size:

A lion can open its mouth
10 inches (25 centimeters).

Biggest

A great white shark's big mouth has 300 sharp teeth. If a tooth breaks, another tooth moves into its place.

Size:

A great white shark's mouth is about 23 inches (58 centimeters) wide.

Hippopotamuses have
the biggest mouths
of all land animals.
One hippo tooth is as long
as a child's arm.

Size:

A hippopotamus can open
its mouth 4 feet (1.2 meters).

Bowhead whales have

the biggest mouths on earth.

Their huge tongues weigh

1 ton (0.9 metric ton).

Size:

A bowhead whale's mouth
is 8 feet (2.4 meters) wide.

Glossary

pouch — a flap of skin shaped like a bag

scoop — to lift or pick up something

snout — the long front part of an animal's face; the snout includes the nose, mouth, and jaws.

swallow — to make food or drink travel from the mouth to the stomach

throat — the front part of the neck

Read More

Bredeson, Carmen. *Great White Sharks Up Close.* Zoom in on Animals! Berkeley Heights, N.J.: Enslow Elementary, 2006.

Fielder, Julie. *Cobras.* Scary Snakes. New York: PowerKids Press, 2008.

Pohl, Kathleen. *Pelicans.* Let's Read about Animals. Milwaukee: Weekly Reader Early Learning Library, 2007.

Internet Sites

FactHound offers a safe, fun way to find Internet sites related to this book. All of the sites on FactHound have been researched by our staff.

Here's all you do:

Visit *www.facthound.com*

FactHound will fetch the best sites for you!

Index

Word Count: 145

Grade: 1

Early-Intervention Level: 12